Suzuki

VIOLIN SCHOOL

Volume 7
Piano Accompaniment
International Edition

AMPV: 1.01

© Copyright 2019, 2014 International Suzuki Association
Sole publisher for the entire world except Japan:
Summy-Birchard, Inc.
Exclusive print rights administered by Alfred Music
All rights reserved. Printed in USA

ISBN-10: 1-4706-1712-9
ISBN-13: 978-1-4706-1712-7

INTRODUCTION

This volume is part of the worldwide Suzuki Method of teaching. The companion recording should be used along with each volume.

For the parent: Credentials are essential for any Suzuki teacher you choose. We recommend that you ask your teacher for his or her credentials, especially relating to training in the Suzuki Method. The Suzuki Method experience should foster a positive relationship among teacher, parent and child. Choosing the right teacher is of the utmost importance.

For the teacher: To be an effective teacher ongoing study and education are essential. Each Regional Suzuki Association provides Teacher Training and Teacher Development for members. It is strongly recommended that all teachers be members of their regional or country associations.

To obtain more information about your Regional Suzuki Association, contact the International Suzuki Association: www.internationalsuzuki.org

This revised edition of the Suzuki Violin School was made by and is a continuing cooperative effort of the International Suzuki Violin Committee using Dr. Shinichi Suzuki's texts and methodology.

EINLEITUNG

Dieses Heft ist Teil der weltweit verbreiteten „Suzuki-Methode". Die dazugehörende Aufnahme sollte stets mit verwendet werden.

Für die Eltern: Jede(r) Suzuki-Lehrer(in) sollte eine entsprechende Ausbildung nachweisen können. Wir empfehlen Ihnen deshalb, Ihre Lehrperson nach ihrer Suzuki-Ausbildung zu fragen. Der Suzuki-Unterricht sollte eine gute Beziehung zwischen Eltern, Kind und Lehrperson fördern. Die Wahl des richtigen Lehrers bzw. der richtigen Lehrerin ist deswegen von höchster Bedeutung.

Für die Lehrer: Um erfolgreich unterrichten zu können, ist ständige Weiterbildung unabdingbar. Jede Nationale Suzuki-Gesellschaft bietet Möglichkeiten zur Aus- und Weiterbildung an. Es ist sehr zu empfehlen, dass alle Suzuki-Lehrer ihrer Nationalen Suzuki-Vereinigung angehören.

Für weitere Informationen: www.internationalsuzuki.org

Diese überarbeitete Ausgabe wurde vom Internationalen Suzuki Komitee für Violine erstellt auf der Grundlage von Dr. Shinichi Suzukis Notentext und seiner Methode.

INTRODUCTION

Ces matériaux appartiennent à la Méthode Suzuki telle qu'elle est enseignée dans les différents pays du monde. Les enregistrements accompagnants doivent être utilisés en combinaison avec cette publication.

Pour les parents: Les qualifications sont essentielles dans le choix du professeur. Aussi nous vous recommandons de demander au professeur quels sont ses diplômes et notamment ceux qui ont trait à l'enseignement de la Méthode Suzuki. L'apprentissage par la Méthode Suzuki doit être une expérience positive, où il existe une relation épanouissante entre l'enfant, le parent et le professeur. Le choix du bon professeur est dès lors d'une importance cruciale.

Pour le professeur: Afin d'enseigner d'une manière efficace selon la pédagogie instrumentale Suzuki, une formation est exigée. Votre association Suzuki régionale ou nationale peut vous offrir une telle formation si vous en êtes membre. Les professeurs sont encouragés à adhérer à leur association Suzuki régionale ou nationale.

De plus amples informations concernant l'Association Suzuki dans votre région peuvent être obtenues sur le site de l'Association Internationale de Suzuki: www.internationalsuzuki.org

La révision de cette édition de l'Ecole Suzuki du Violon a été réalisée par le comité de l'Association Internationale Suzuki pour le violon, en utilisant les textes et la méthodologie du docteur Shinichi Suzuki.

INTRODUCCIÓN

Este material es parte del mundialmente conocido Método Suzuki de enseñanza. Las grabaciones complementarias deben ser usadas con estas publicaciones.

Para los padres: Es importante que el profesor que escojan tenga certificados de estudios. Recomendamos que pidan al profesor que muestre dichos documentos, especialmente aquellos relacionados con el Método Suzuki. La experiencia de aprender con el Método Suzuki debe ser única y positiva para los alumnos, en la que exista una maravillosa y estrecha relación entre el niño, el padre y el maestro. Por eso es de mayor importancia escoger al maestro adecuado.

Para el maestro: Para ser un maestro Suzuki de calidad, se requiere de una preparación intensa y constante. Las asociaciones Suzuki de cada región proveen de dicha preparación a sus miembros. Es fuertemente recomendable que los profesores sean miembros de la asociación Suzuki de su país y de la asociación Suzuki de su región.

Para obtener más información acerca del Método Suzuki en su país, por favor contacten con la Asociación Internacional Suzuki: www.internationalsuzuki.org

Esta edición revisada del Método Suzuki de Violín ha sido realizada por el Comité Internacional de Violín Suzuki, basándose en los textos y metodología del Dr. Shinichi Suzuki.

CONTENTS

Page

| 1 | Minuet/Menuet/Menuett/Minueto, *W. A. Mozart*..4 |

| 2 | Courante, *A. Corelli* ....7 |

| 3 | Sonata in A Major, HWV 361, *G. F. Handel*..9 |
Sonate en la Majeur, HWV 361
Sonate in A-Dur, HMV 361
Sonata en la mayor, HWV 361

| 4 | Concerto in A Minor, BWV 1041, *J. S. Bach*..17 |
Concerto en la mineur, BWV 1041
Konzert in a-Moll, BWV 1041
Concierto en la menor, BWV 1041

| 5 | Allegro, *A. Corelli*..38 |

1 Minuet

Menuet   Menuett   Minueto

W. A. Mozart

6

2 Courante

A. Corelli

3 Sonata in A Major, HWV 361

Sonate en la Majeur, HWV 361   Sonate in A-Dur, HMV 361   Sonata en la mayor, HWV 361

G. F. Handel

4 Concerto in A Minor, BWV 1041

Concerto en la mineur, BWV 1041   Konzert in a-Moll, BWV 1041   Concierto en la menor, BWV 1041

J. S. Bach

* As there are no dynamic markings in Bach's manuscripts for the Concerto, the Gigue, or the Courante, the suggested dynamics are indicated in parentheses.
* Les partitions manuscrites de Bach pour le Concerto, la Gigue et la Courante ne comportent aucune indications de nuances, celles suggérées ici figurent entre parenthèses.
* Da es keine dynamischen Zeichen in Bachs Manuskripten für dieses Konzert, die Gigue und die Courante gibt, sind die Dynamik-Vorschläge in Klammern angegeben.
* Como no hay indicaciones de dinámica en los manuscritos del Concierto, la Giga y la *Courante* de Bach, las dinámicas sugeridas están indicadas entre paréntesis.

7 Allegro

A. Corelli